GNOME SWEET GNOME

TWENTY-FIVE UNIQUE ADULT COLORING BOOK DESIGNS TO KEEP YOU ENTERTAINED FOR HOURS

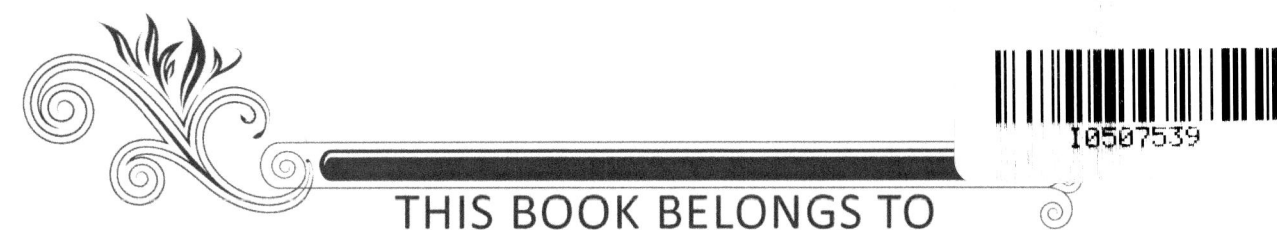

THIS BOOK BELONGS TO

Okay is the life of a jolly wood gnome.
They have long beards and they love your lawn.
They dance little jigs on their little gnome homes.

All rights reserved. No part of this book may be reproduced in any form or by any electronic means including information storage and retrieval systems, without permission in writing from the publisher.

Copyright © 2021 Dawné Dominique
ISBN: 978-1-7750442-8-4
Cover and Art Designed by Dawné Dominique
Vector Stock ©
DepositPhoto ©
IStock ©

Published by DusktilDawn Publications/Designs
CANADA

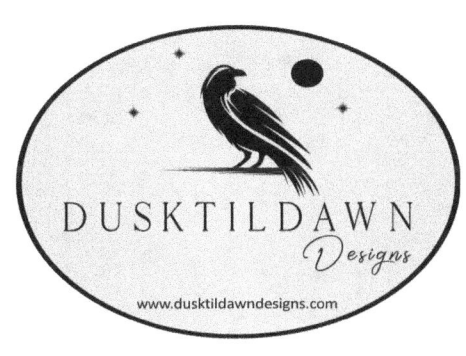

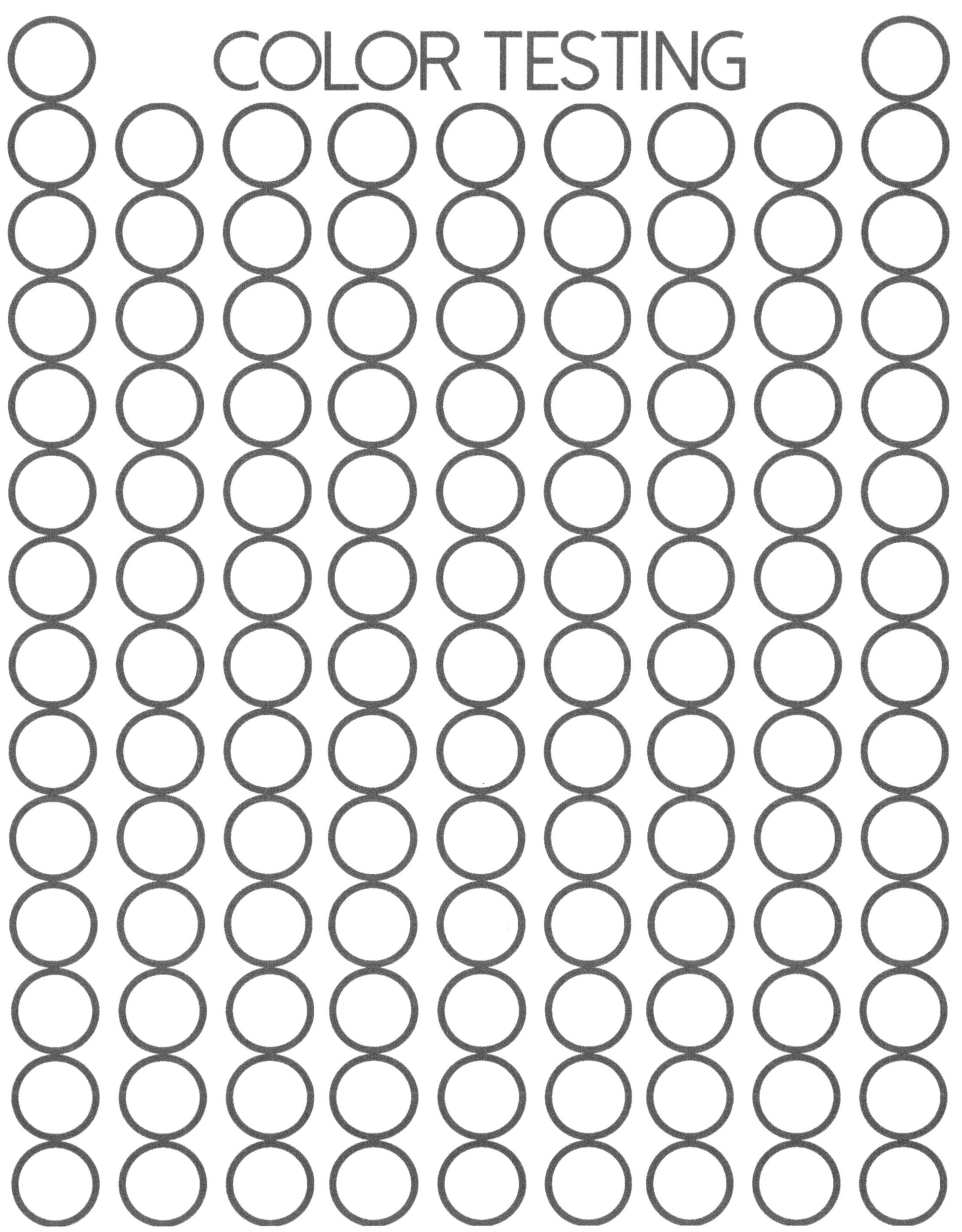

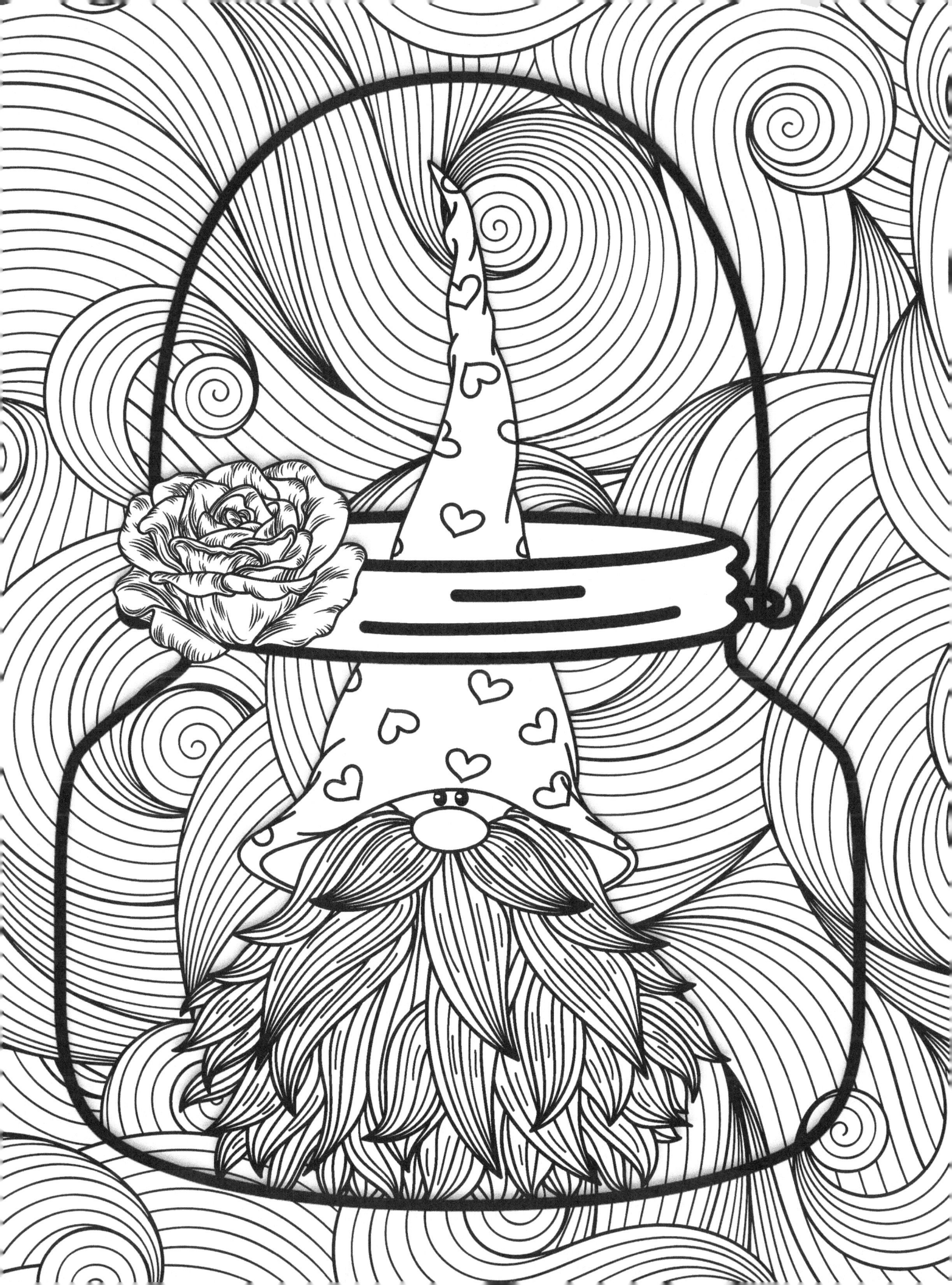

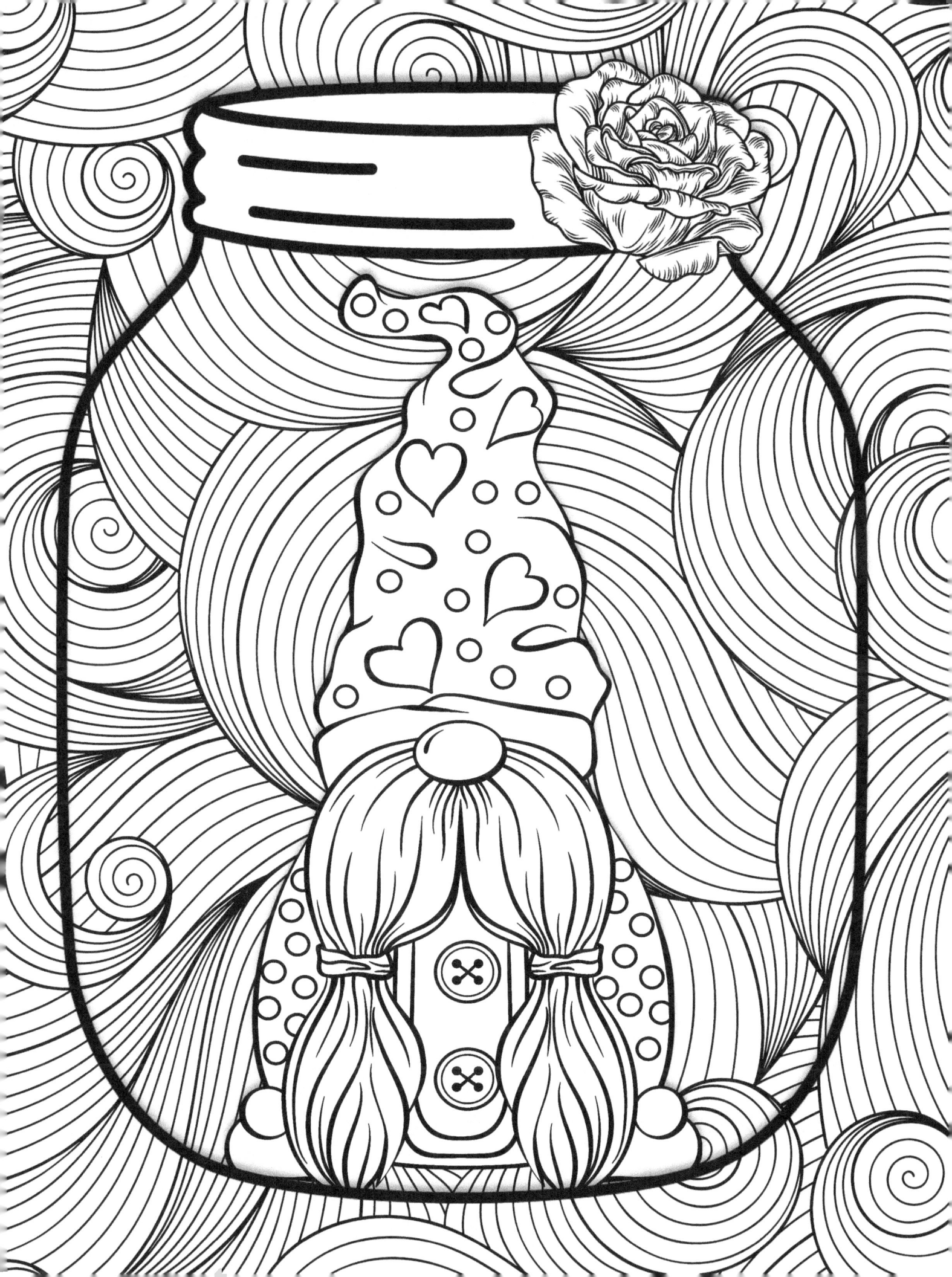

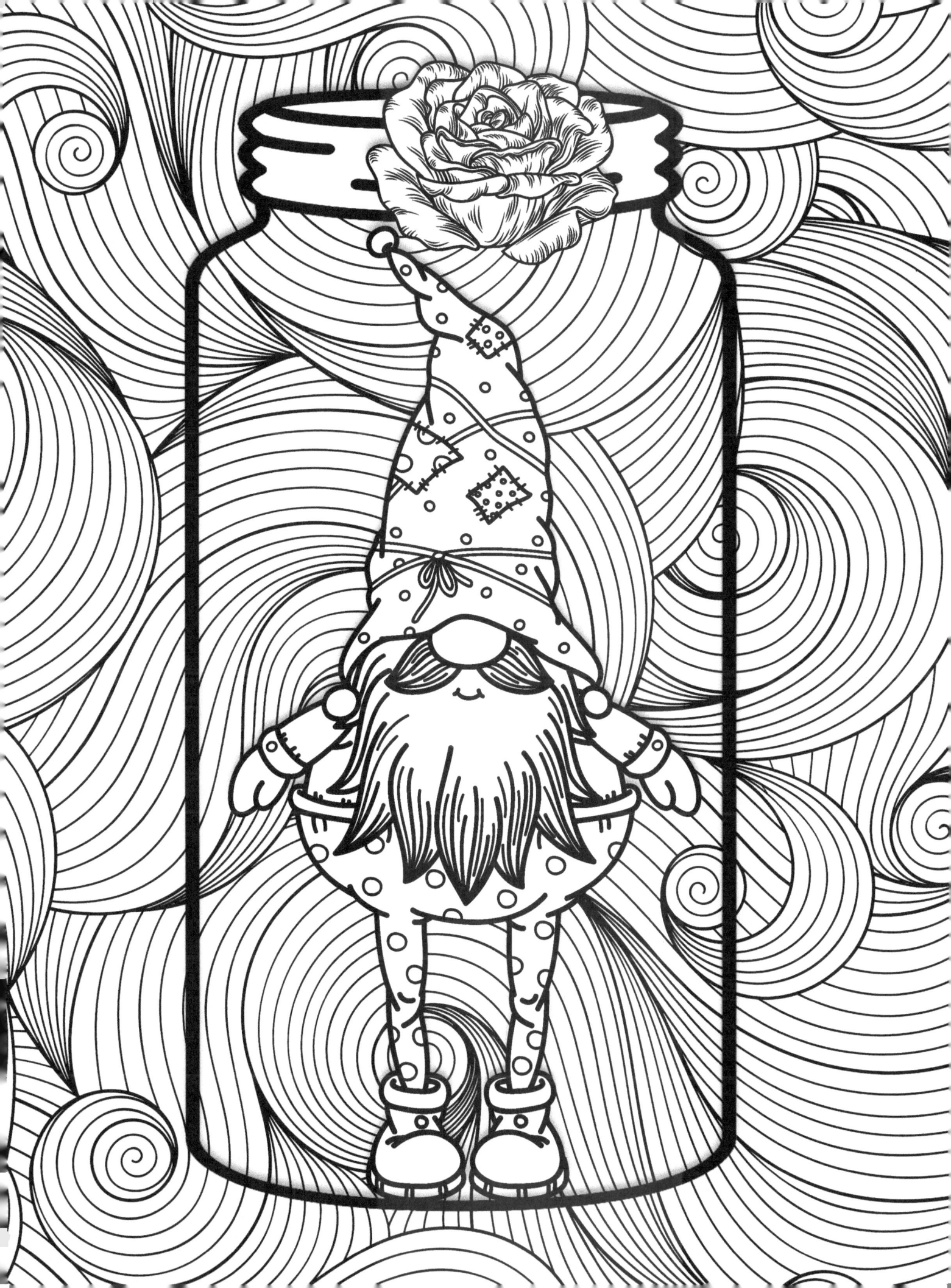

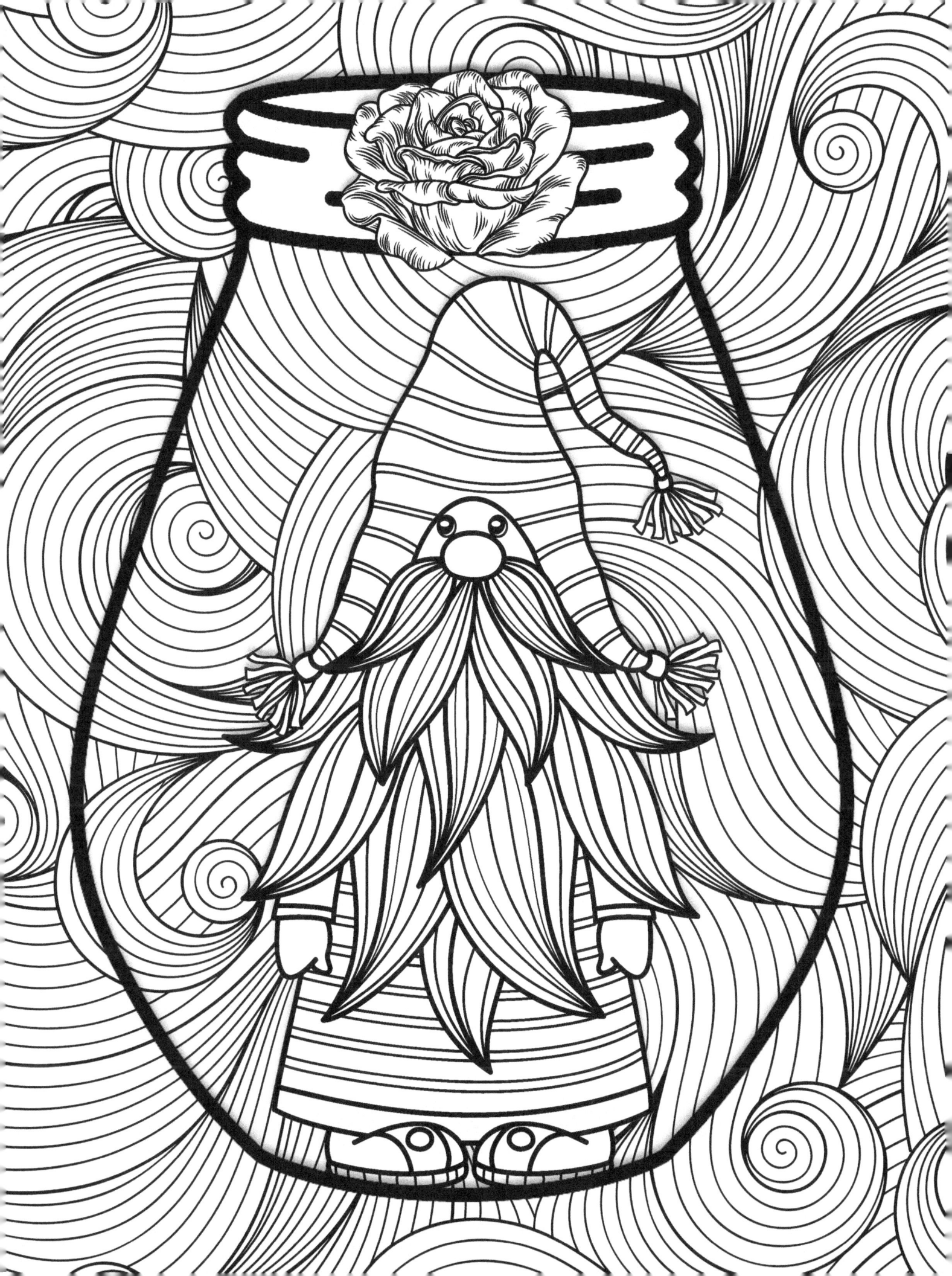

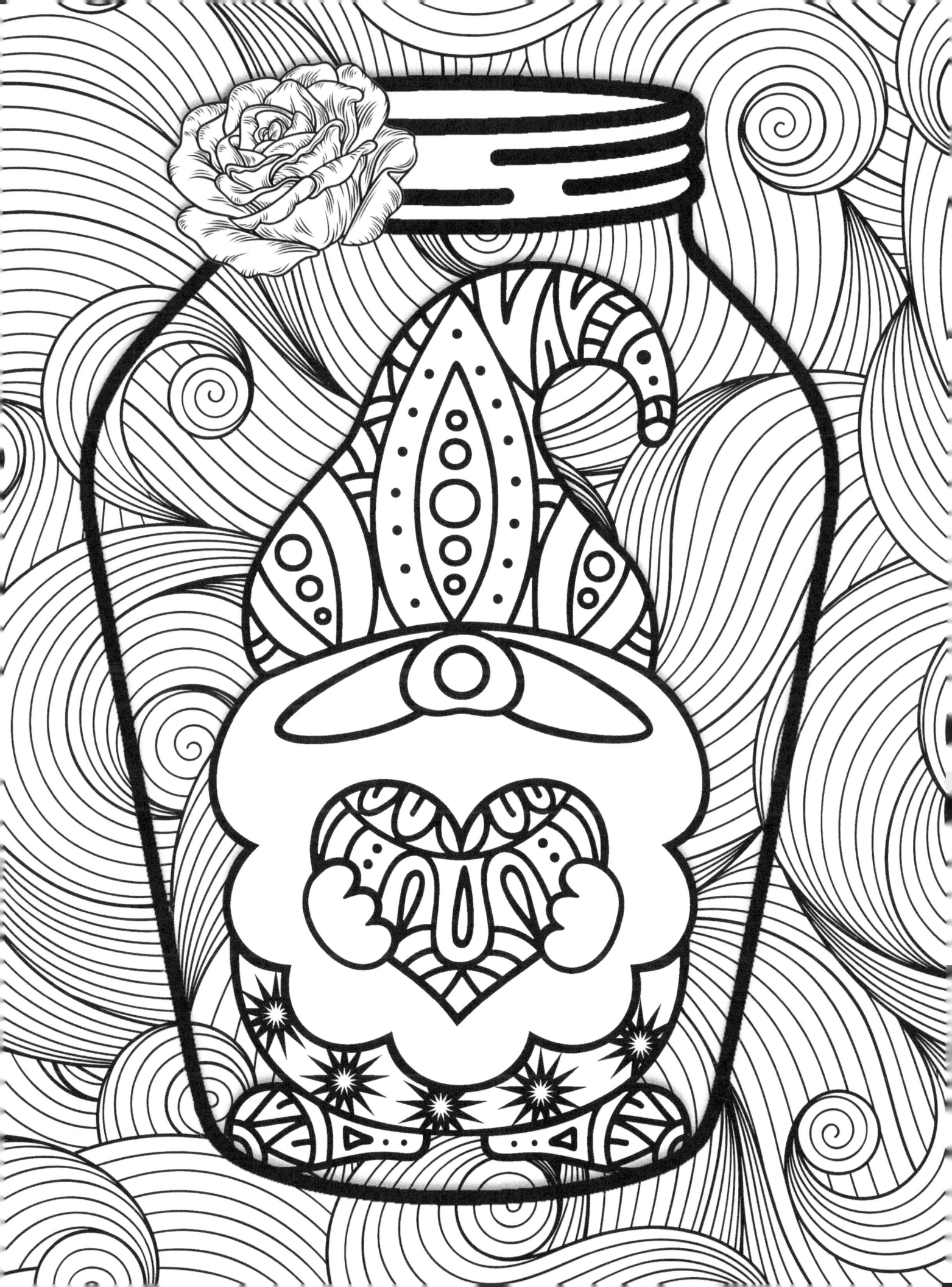

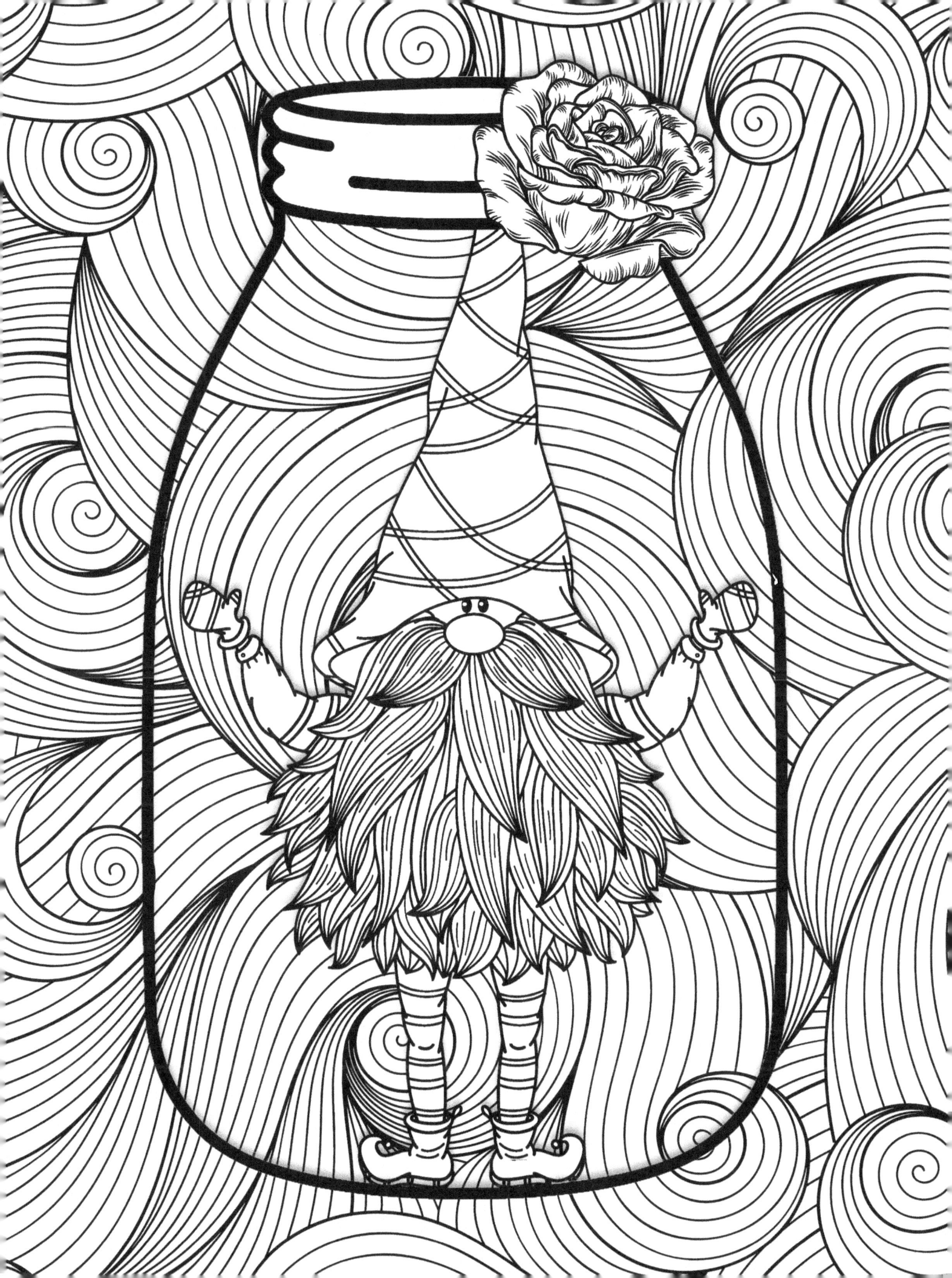

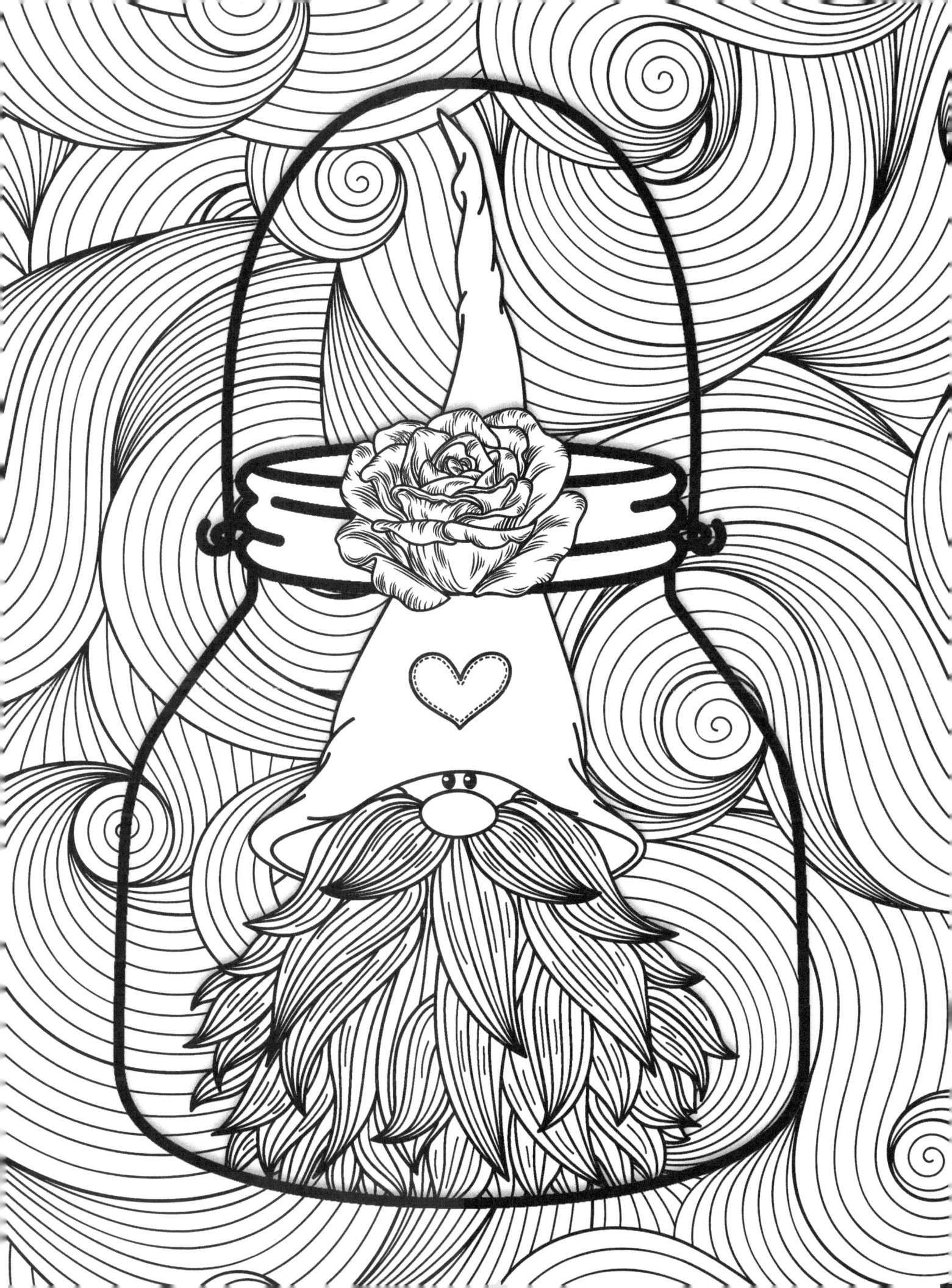

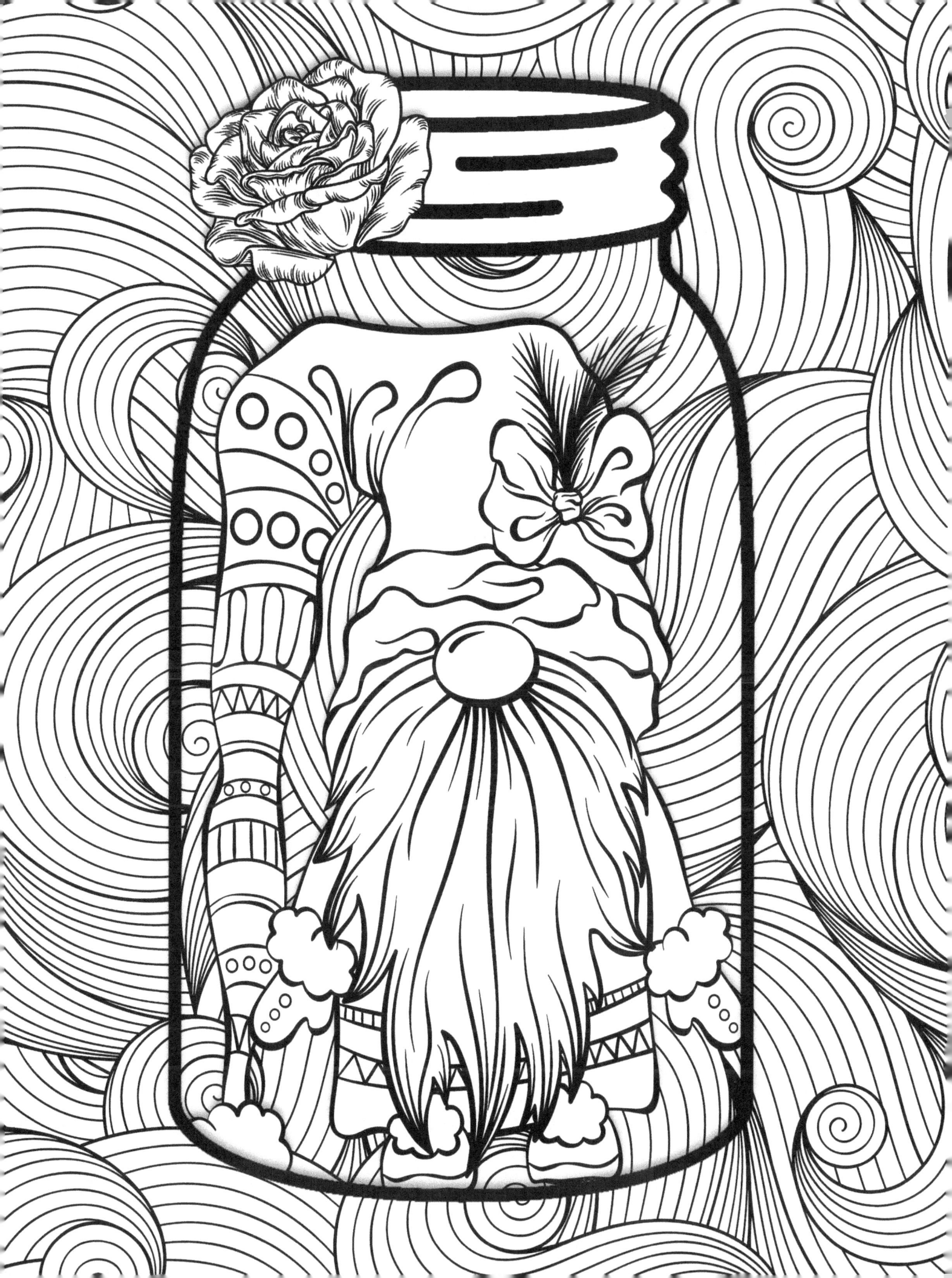

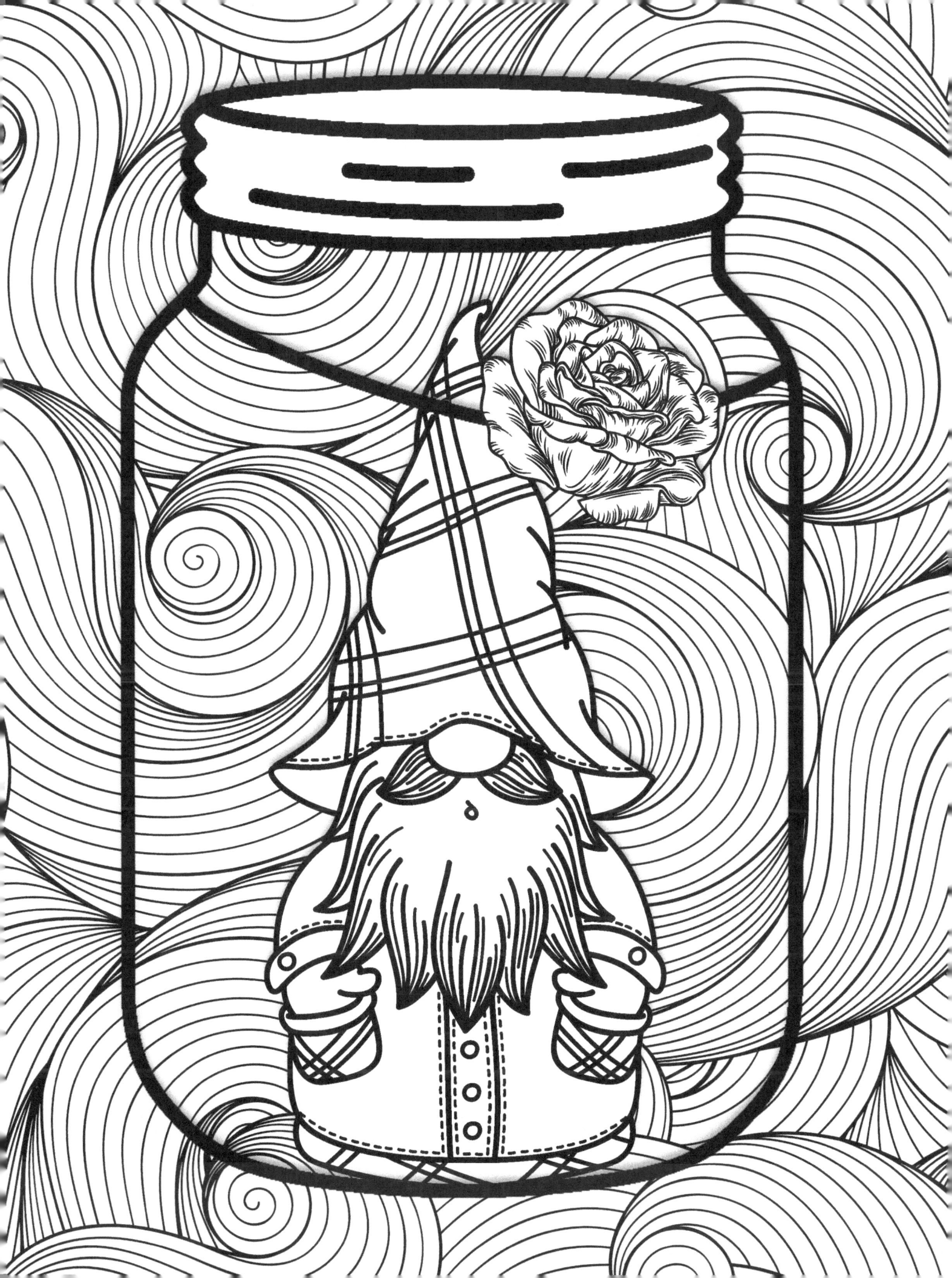

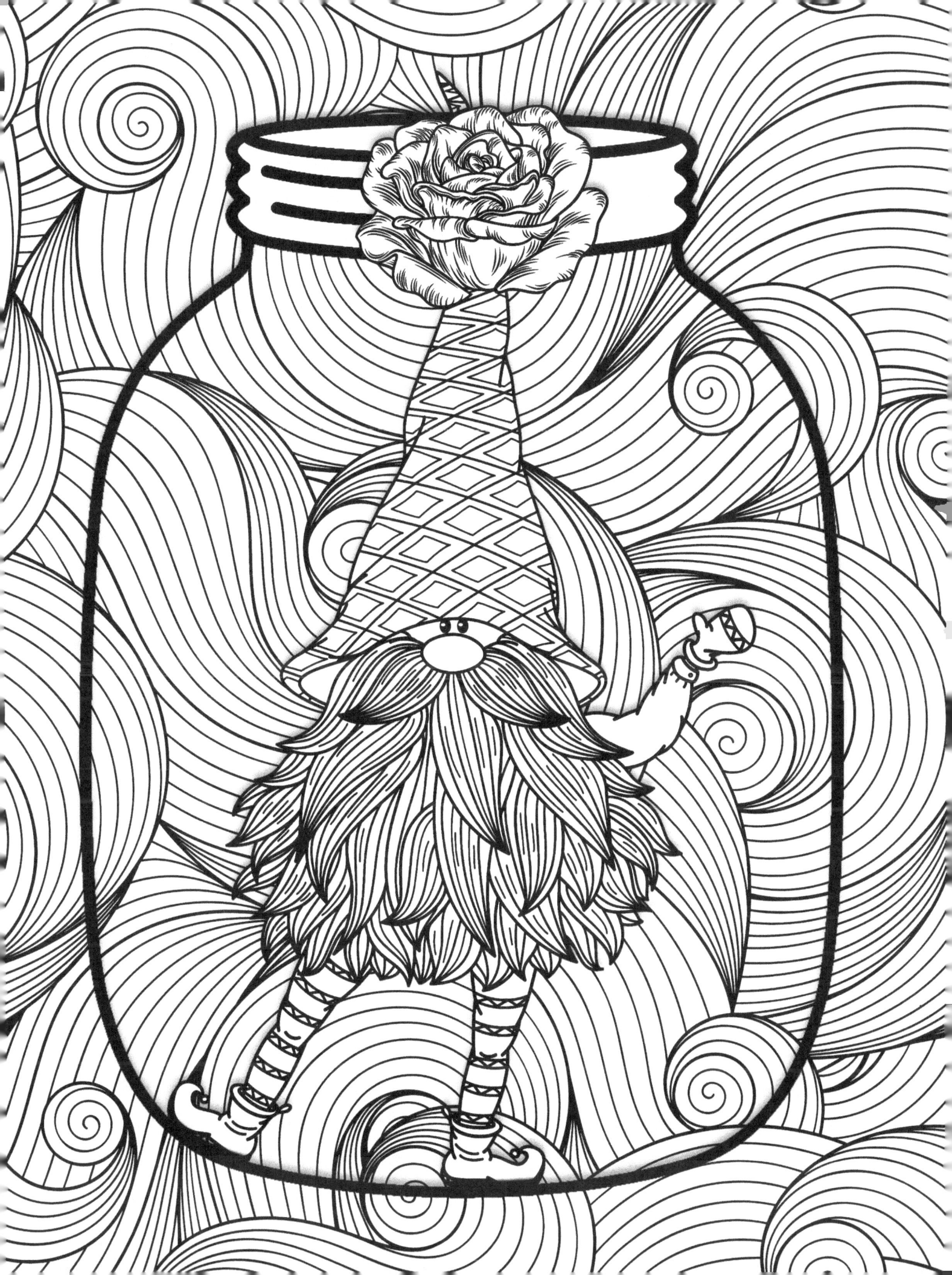

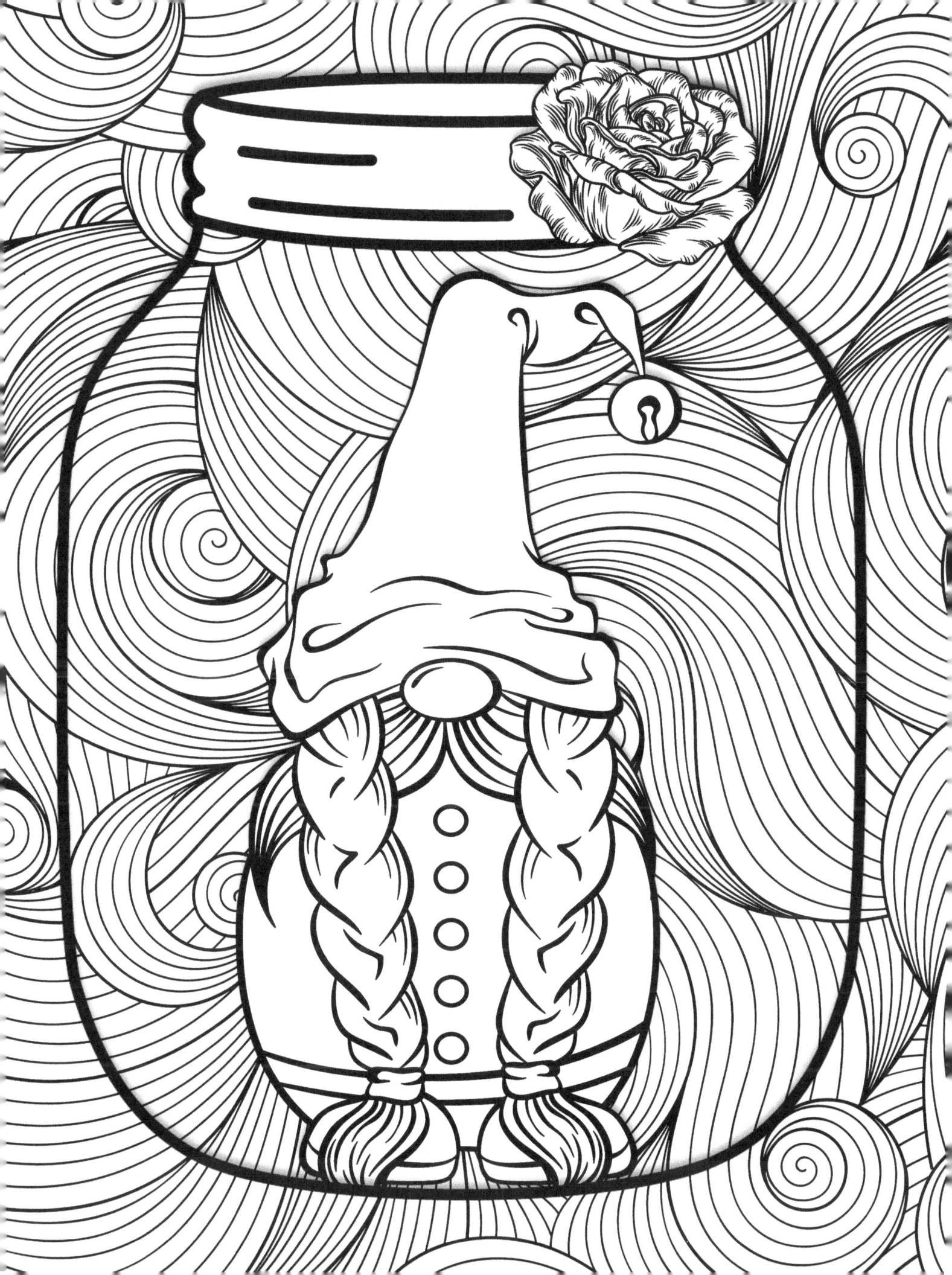

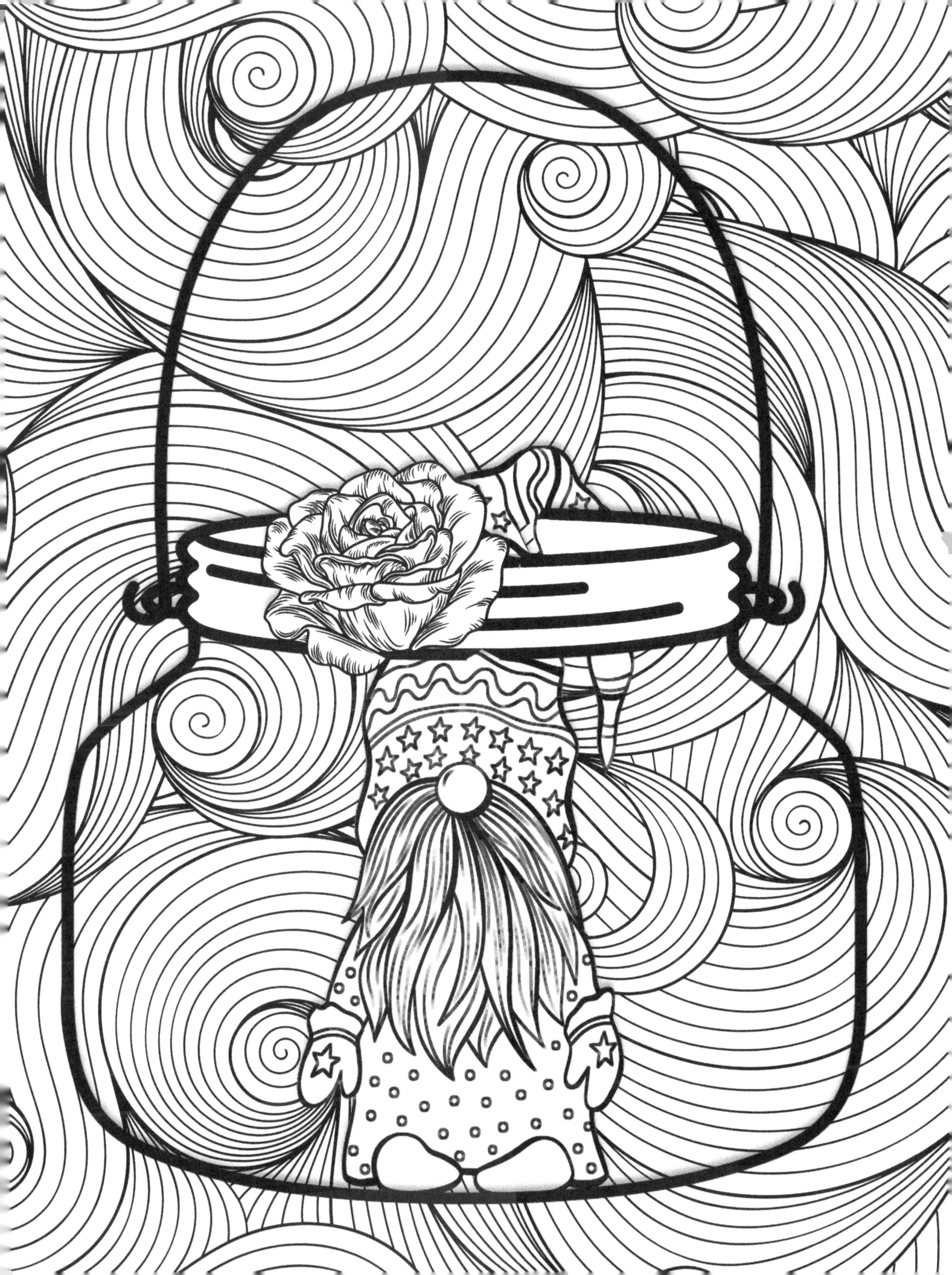

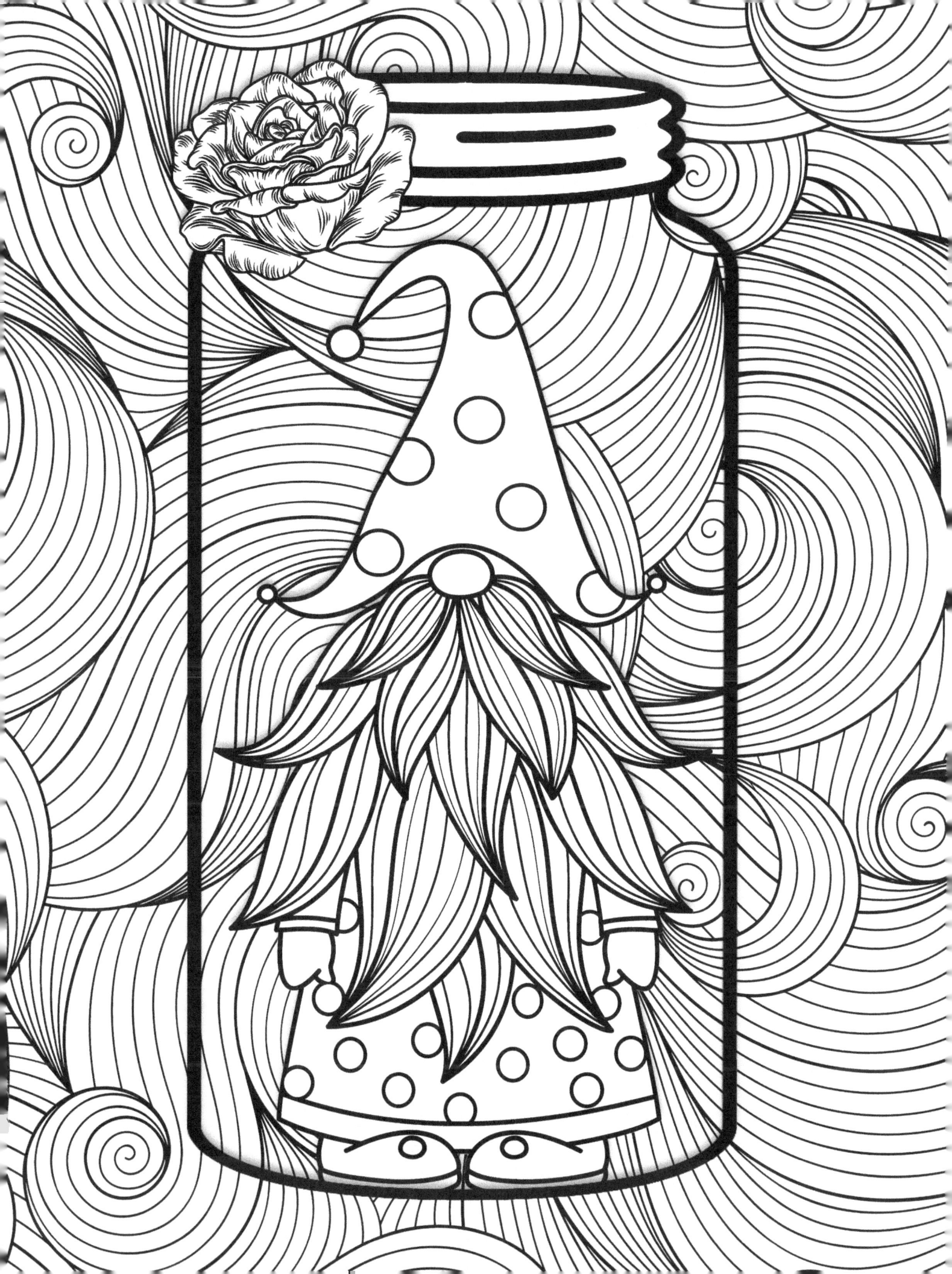

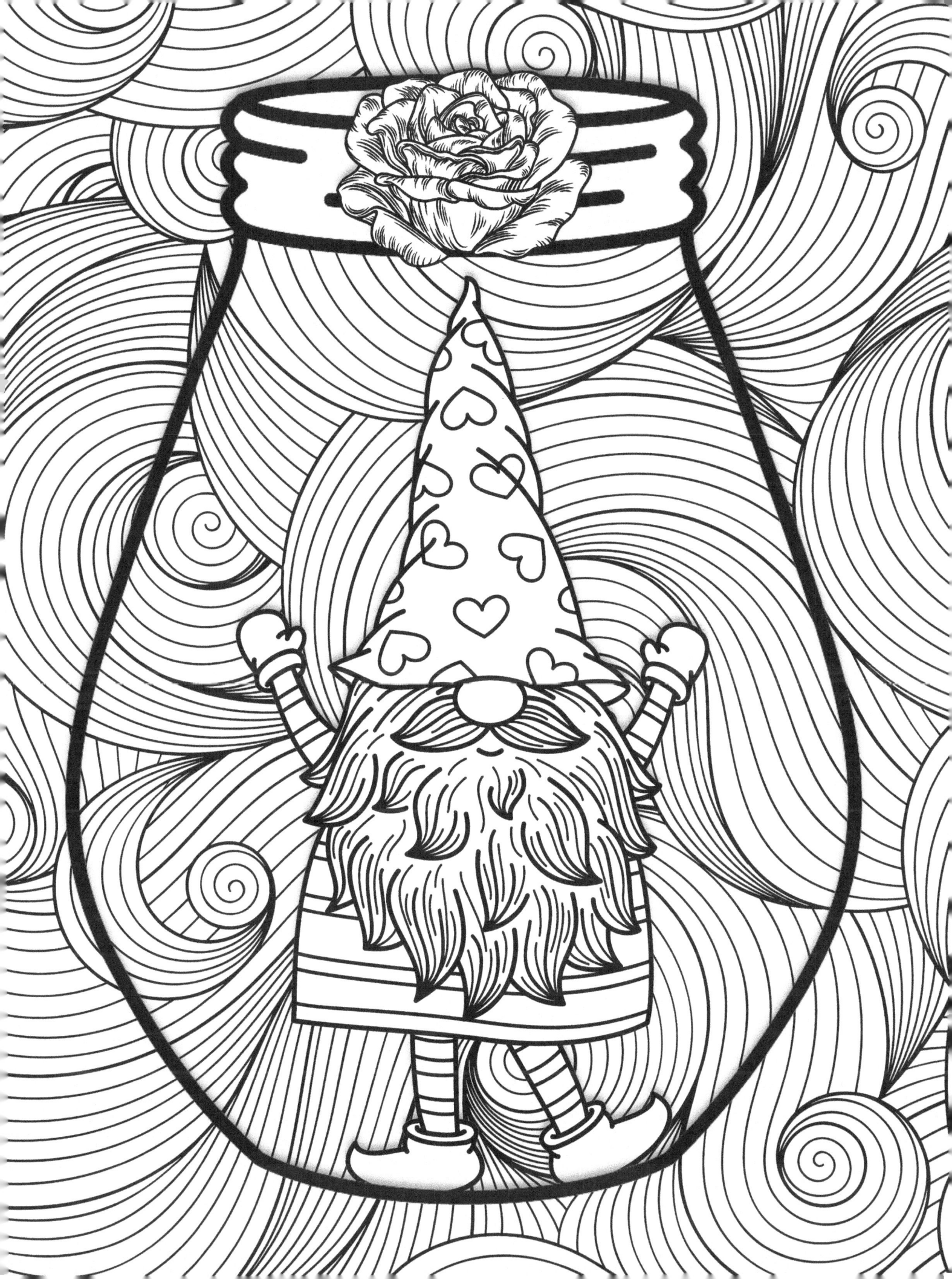

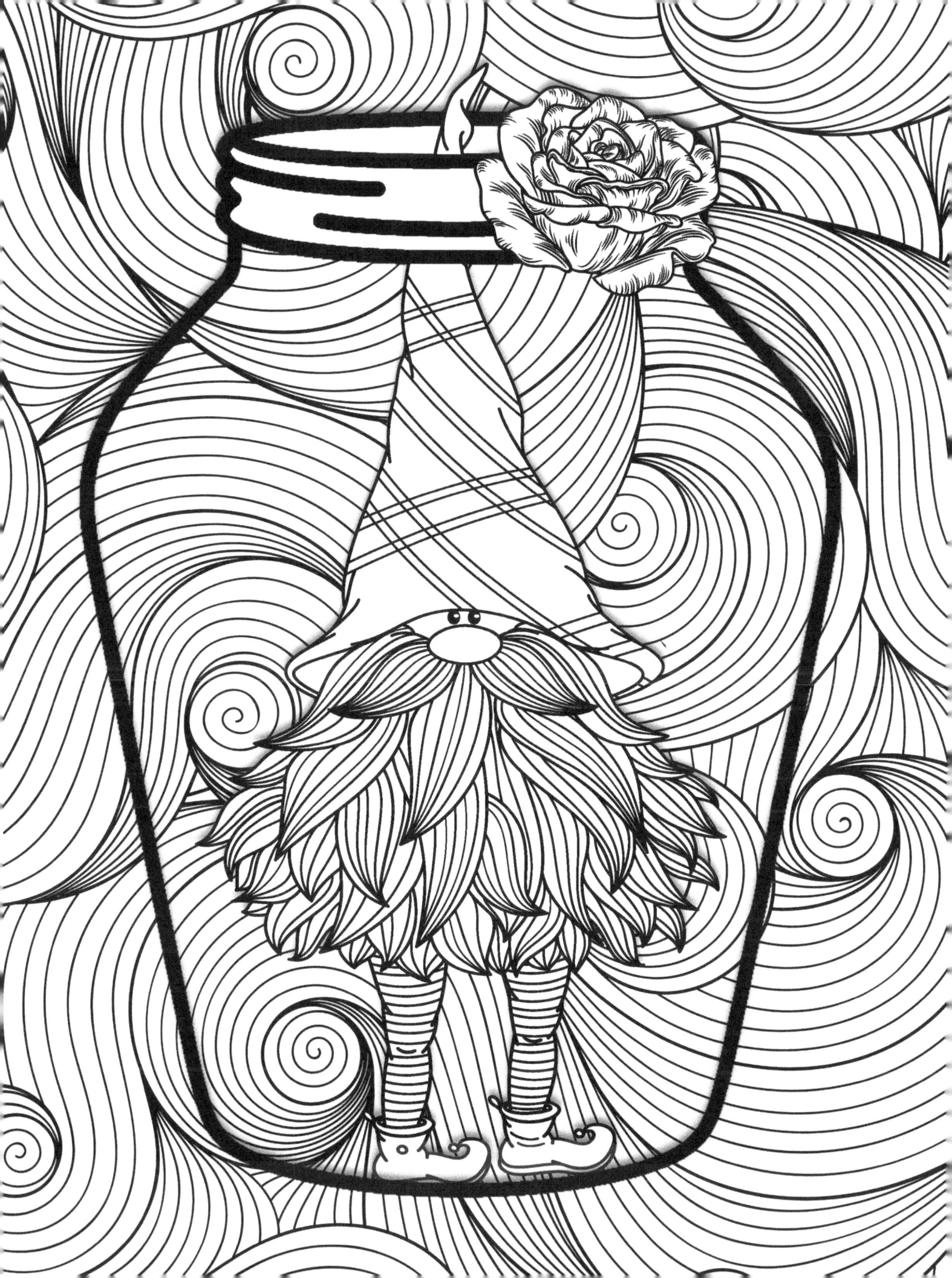

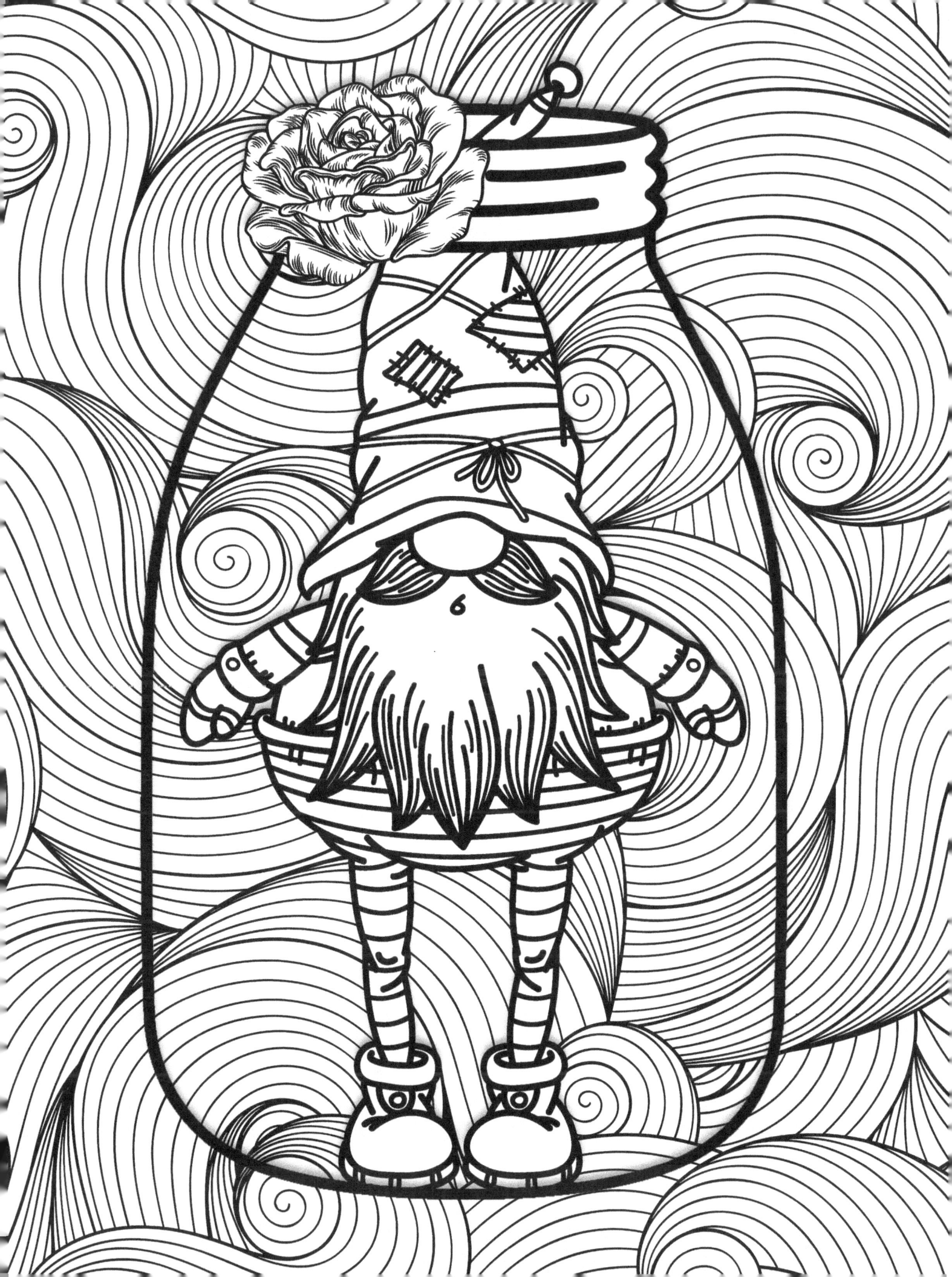

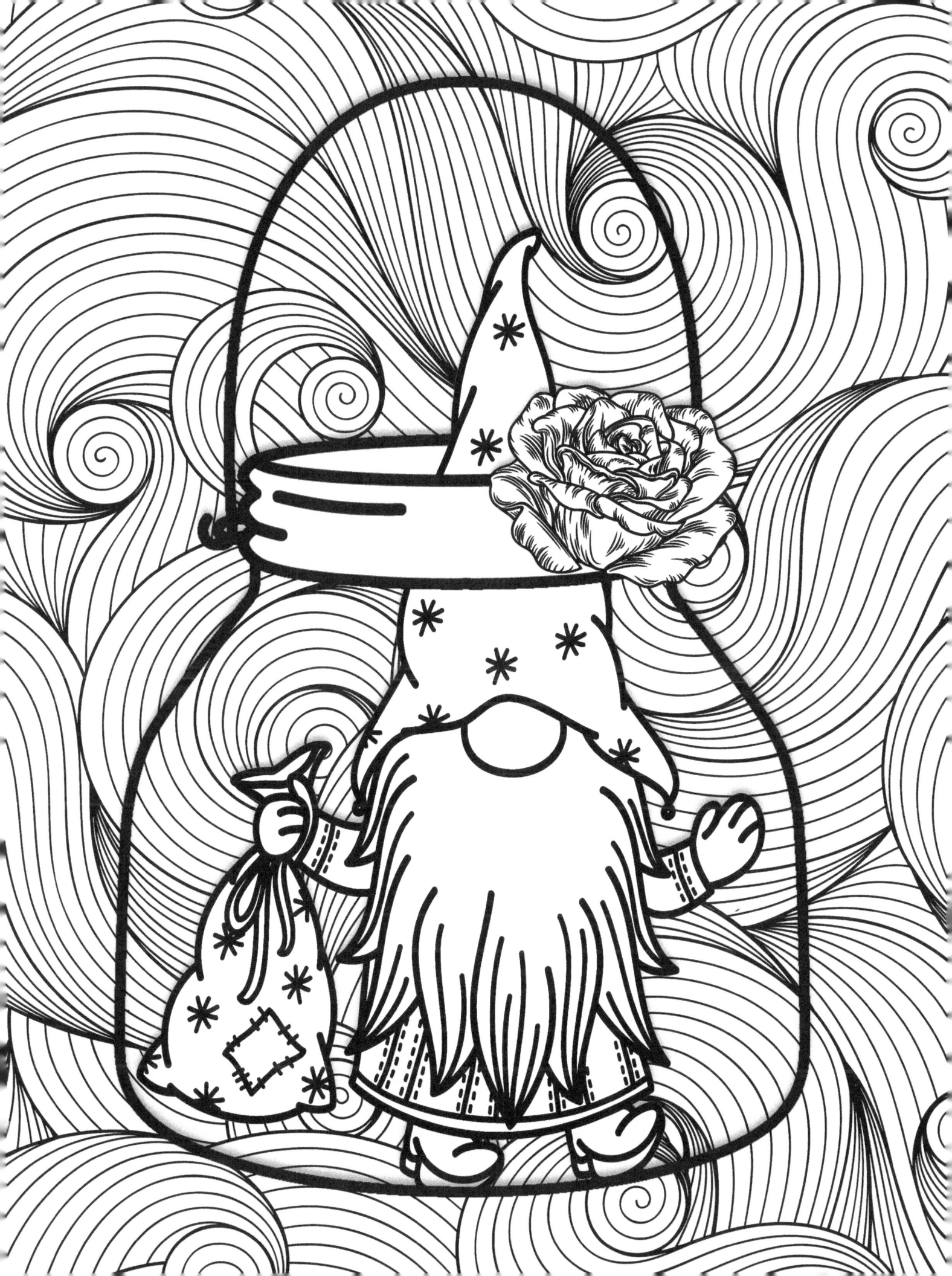

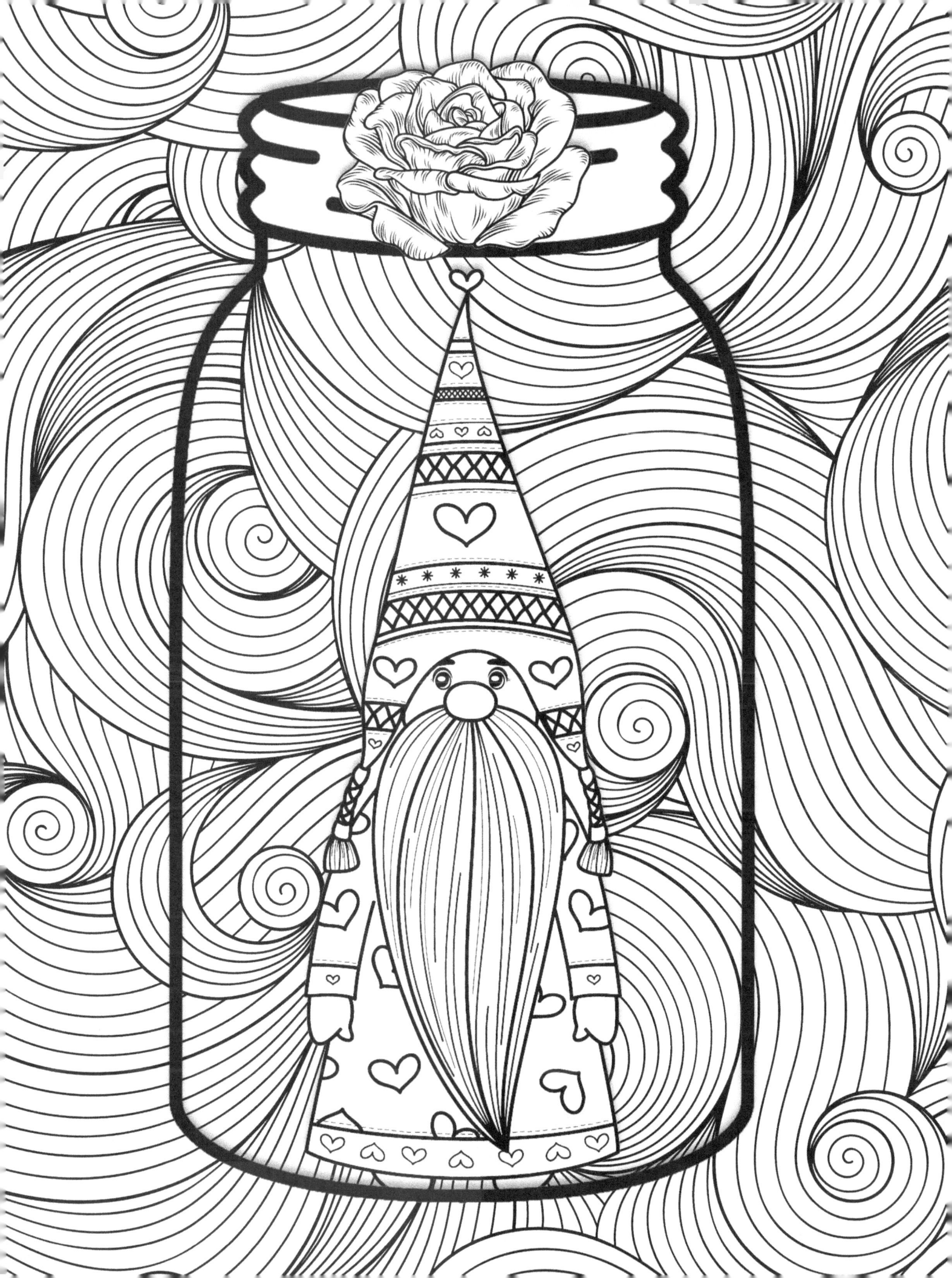

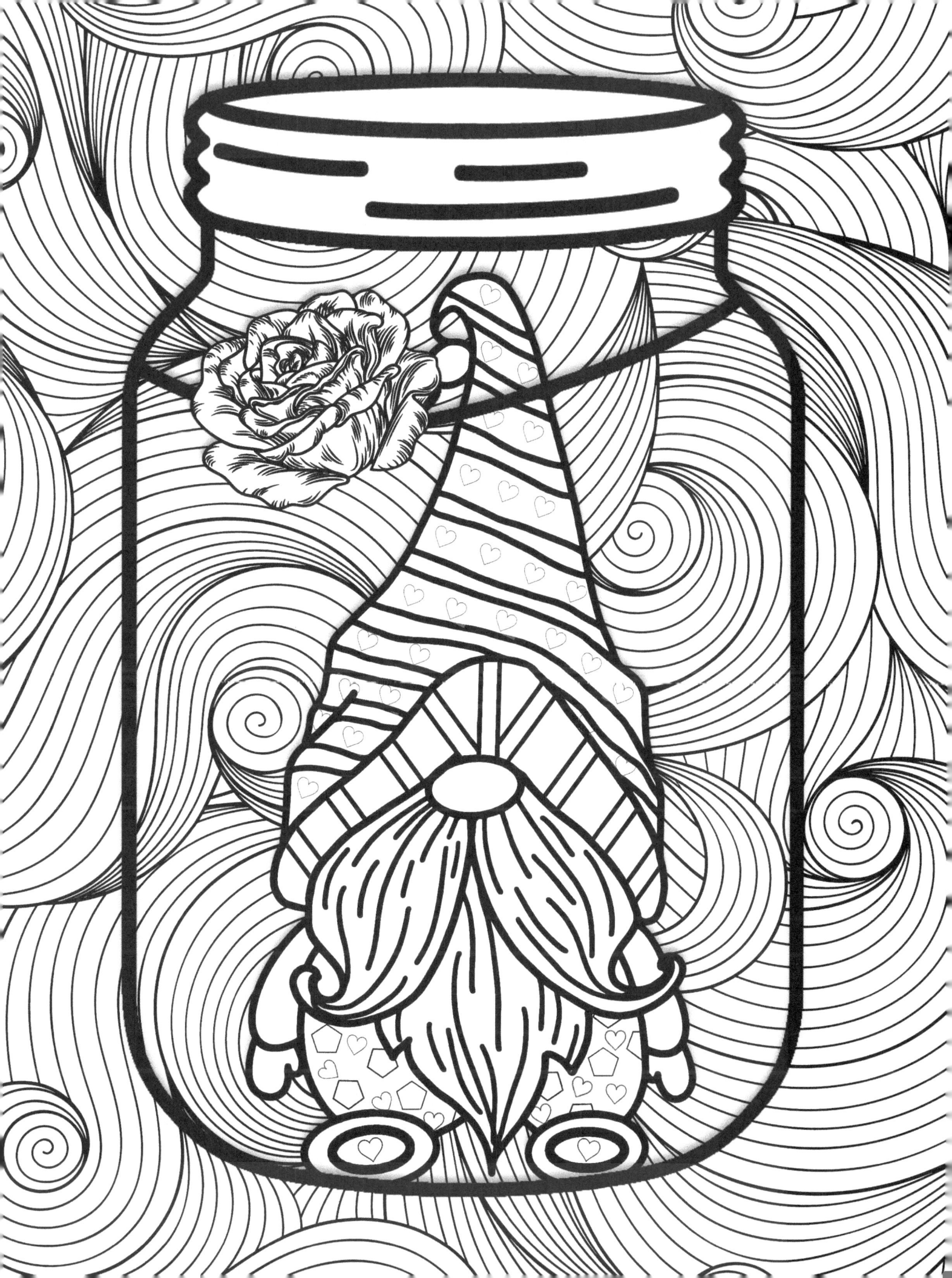

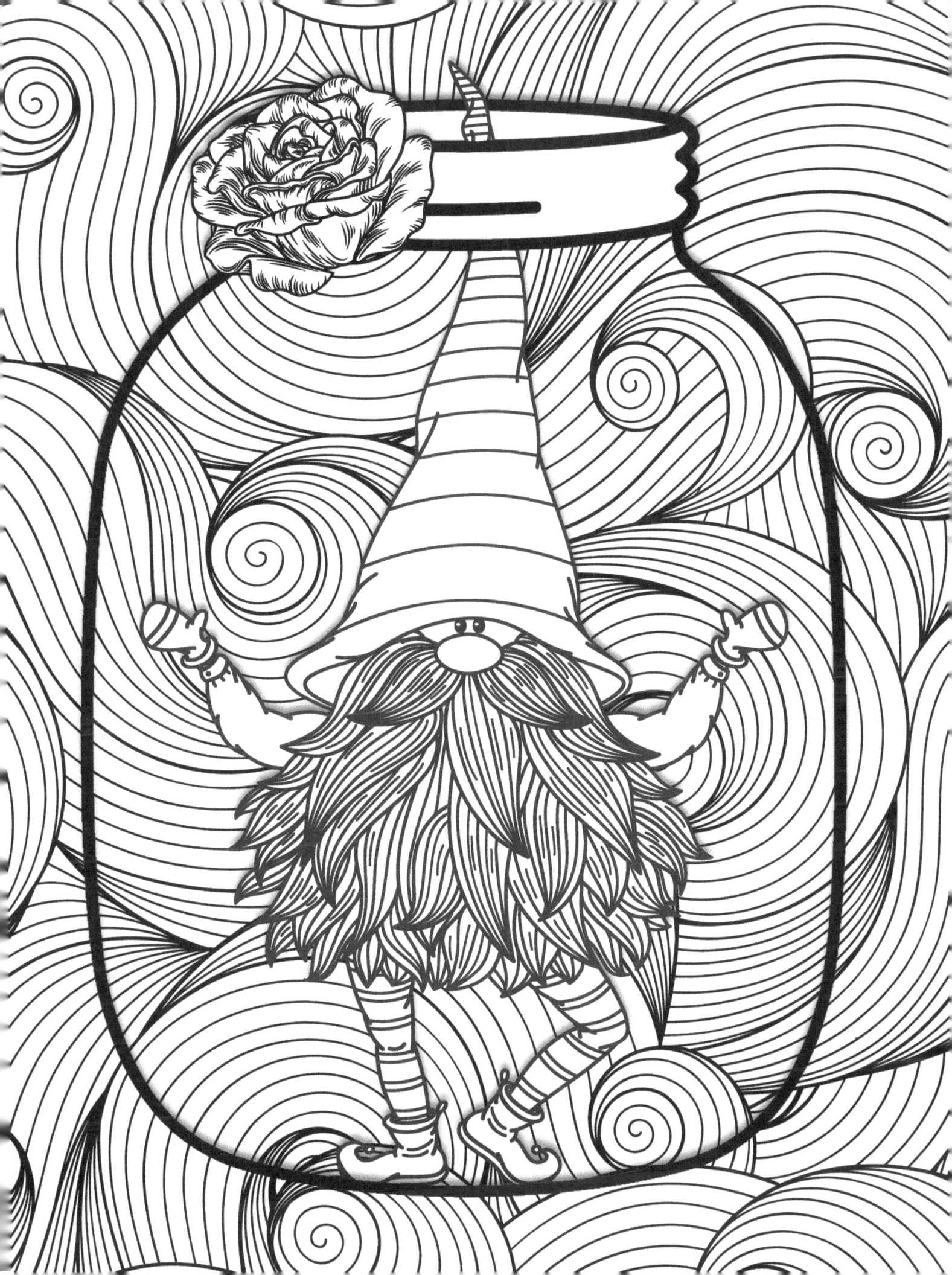

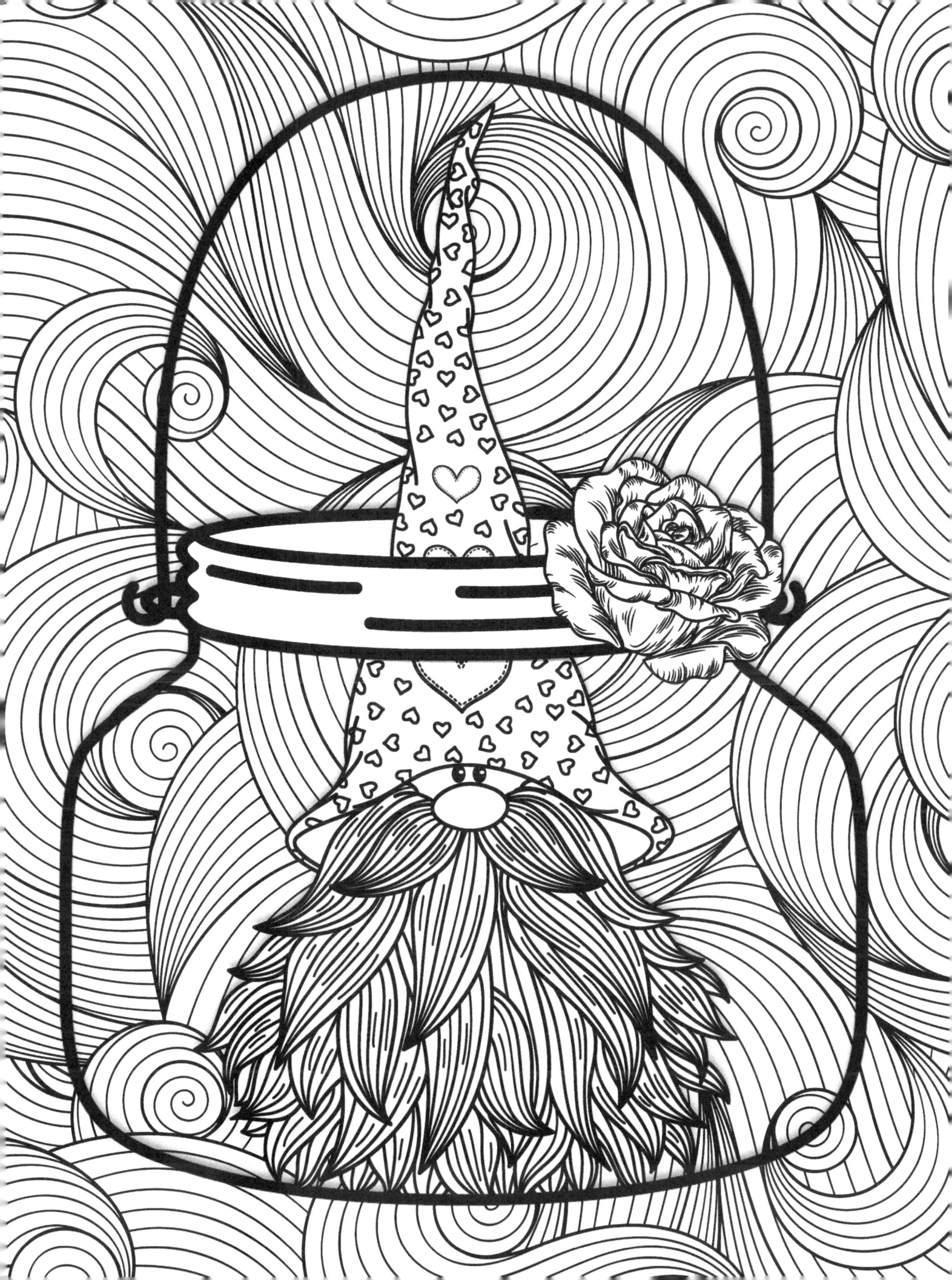

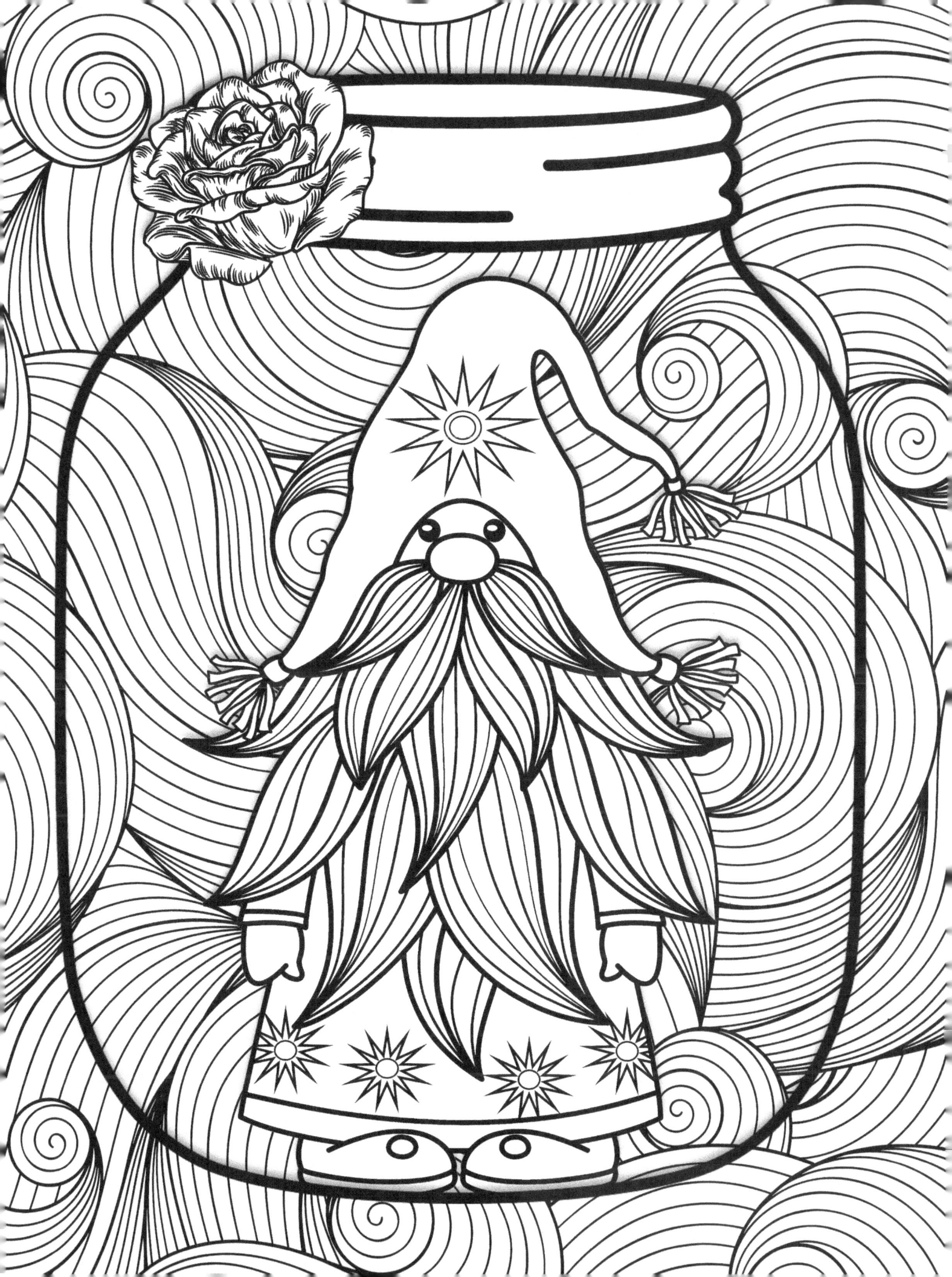

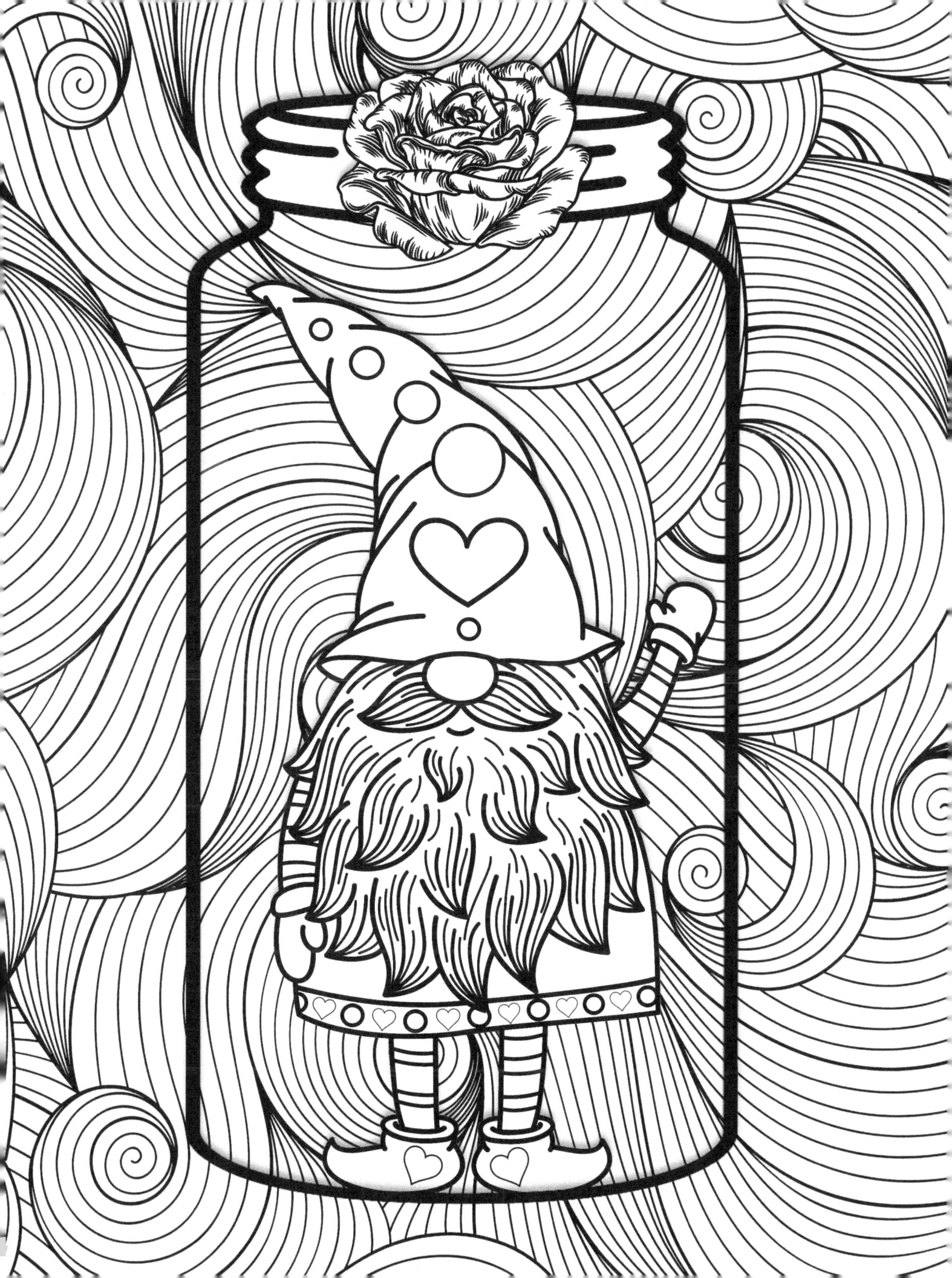

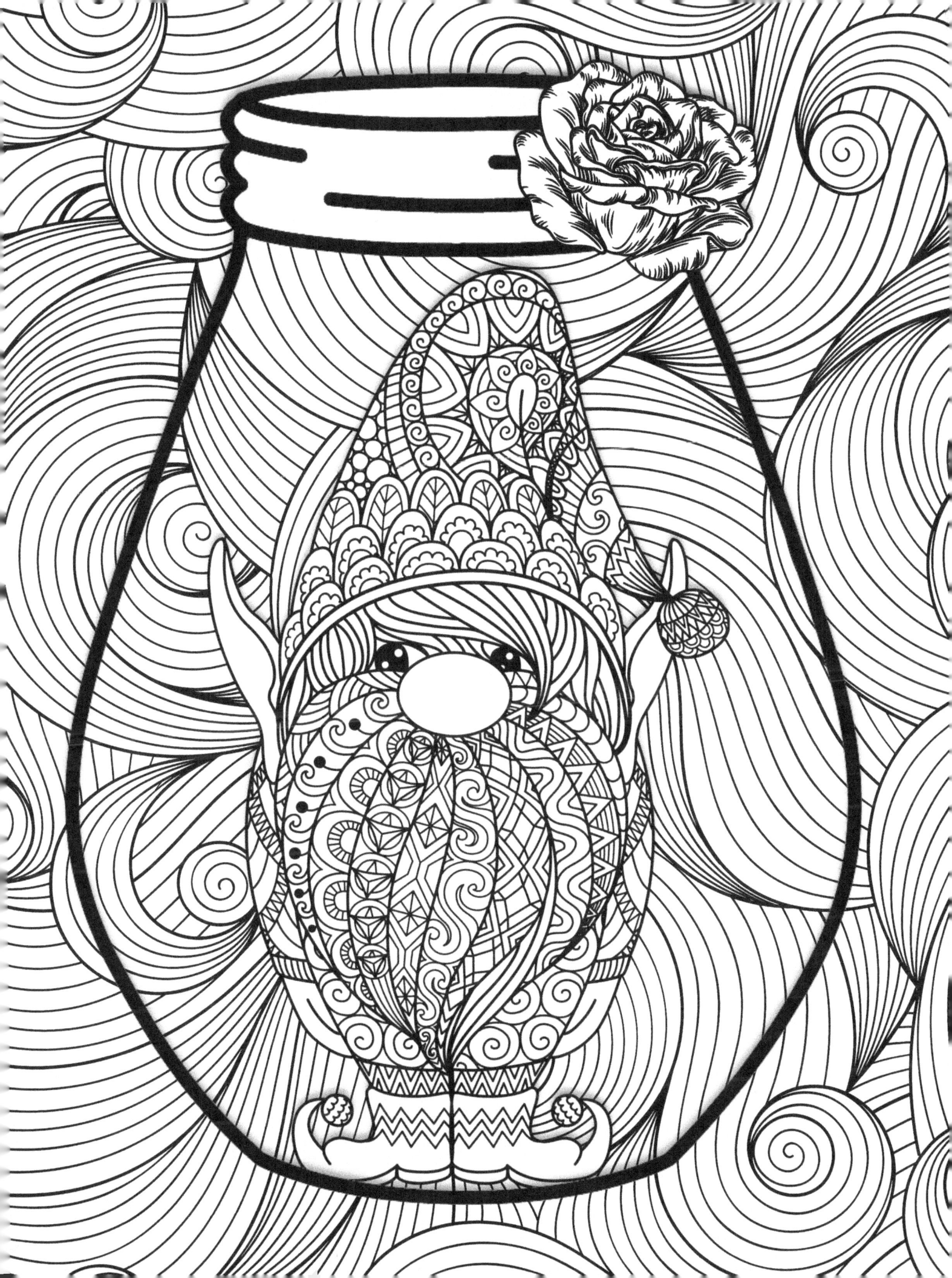

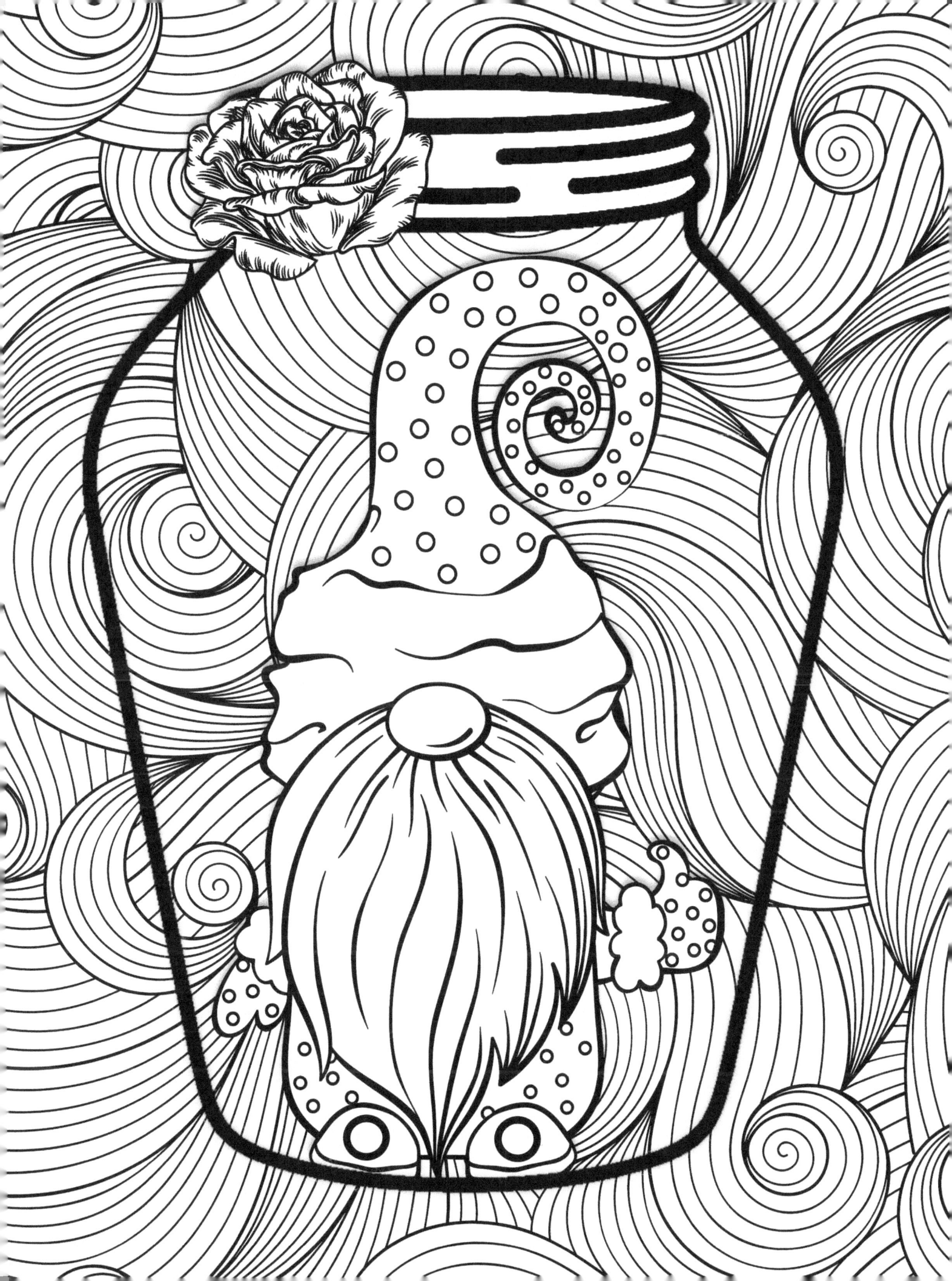

IF YOU ENJOYED THIS COLORING BOOK, DON'T BE SHY...LEAVE A REVIEW.

Check out other adult coloring books by Dawné Dominique & D. Thomas-Jerlo

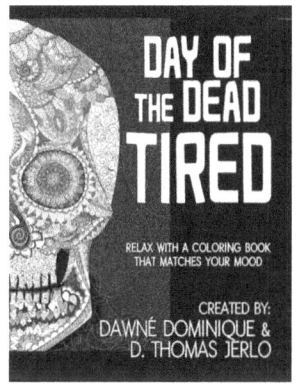 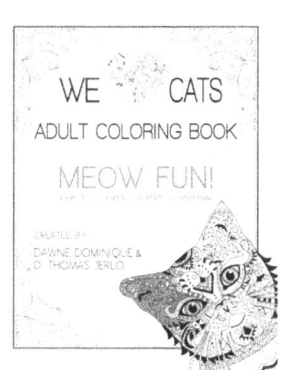 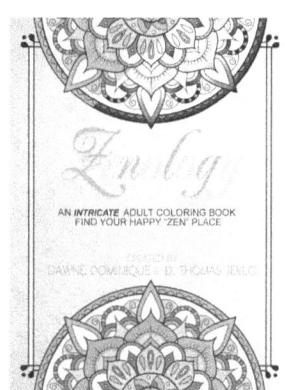 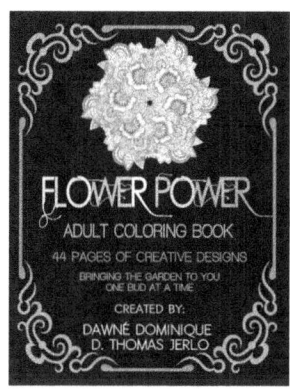

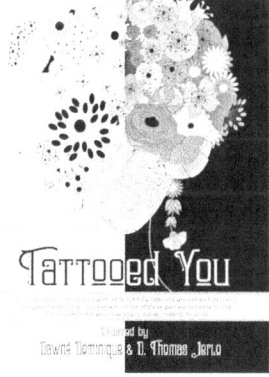

www.lulu.com/spotlight/dusktildawn

Also available at: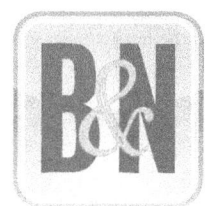